In the Shadow of the Formless

The Lost Writings of Wu Hsin Vol. 3

Translation by Roy Melvyn

In the Shadow of the Formless
The Lost Writings of Wu Hsin Vol. 3
By Roy Melvyn
Copyright 2011 Roy Melvyn

Summa Iru Publishing
Boulder, Colorado 80020

Forward

You hold in your hand a most unique tutorial on the subject of being. In one sense, it is unique in that the subject of how-to-be does not receive much attention. In another sense, its uniqueness rests in the simplicity and clarity in which the subject is presented.

These lost writings of the ancient Chinese Wu Hsin are completely devoid of compromise. They challenge the most fundamental assumptions we make about ourselves and our world and, when viewed from openness, are truly transformative.

In *Volume Three, In the Shadow of the Formless*, Wu Hsin continues his great treatise with some surprising statements. For example:

One inherent error is
The preference for
The song of the future over
The seeming blandness of
The present moment.
Another error is
Using the mind
To try to understand
The words of Wu Hsin.
The mind is a tool
Unsuited to this task.
The proper tool is silence.
The seed is in the ground;
The sun will shine;
The rain will fall;
Nothing need be done.

Nothing need be done. After all the words have been read, after their meaning has been pondered with new concepts possibly added, nothing need be done. How hard this is for the Western mind to accept. "What do I need to do to get it?" is the usual question. Here, Wu Hsin provides the disconcerting answer "Nothing need be done".

Behind this statement lies the even more disquieting question "Who is there to do anything?" Therein, the reader is returned to one of the central themes of Wu Hsin, that is, that there really is no such thing as an individual:

There is a belief of separateness,
That you are separate from the rest.
There is nothing you can do
To rid yourself of this belief because
"You" is the belief.

Stated in modern terms, the philosophy of Wu Hsin could be summed up in this manner:

There is thinking and there is functioning, distinct from thinking.

Thinking reflects the programming for survival, for continuity, which manifests through the psychosomatic apparatus. A reference point is created via the thought me. This me is the sum or totality of all fears: the fear of pain, the fear of loss, and ultimately, the fear of absence. Most of the thoughts regarding me are repetitious, an extraneous feedback loop in the nervous system.

Interestingly however, thought is not born in the brain any more than a radio creates sound. It is merely transmitted through it.

Functioning occurs through the workings of consciousness and the life-force. Functioning is effortless and natural. Cells are replaced, wastes are eliminated, what needs to be done gets done. There is an aware-presence-energy.

Giving attention to thought perpetuates the programming. Giving attention to the functioning, the aware-presence-energy, facilitates the de-programming.

The "I/me" is latent in the apparatus at birth, as the flower is latent in the seed. The preliminary programming is installed genetically.

At some point between 18-24 months, sufficient memories, both pleasant and unpleasant, have accumulated thereby triggering the "I/me" or self consciousness to arise. Seeing itself as separate and insecure causes the activation (boot) of the programming as a means of protection. It is perpetually modified and adjusted (upgraded) by the experiences of the apparatus and is further "tweaked" by the moment-by-moment adjustments made by the endocrine system.

From that point forward, the hardware (soma) receives the input from the environment. It is processed by the software (psyche) which provides the output ([re]action). There is no individual, as such, doing anything. Everything that happens is the cause of everything that happens.

There is no center to infinity.

I strongly doubt that Wu Hsin would want readers to take him at his word. Instead, he would ask that each investigate the matter deeply within oneself. Search for the individual, locate the operating center.

This is the lasting challenge of one of the most profound teachers of all time.

Brief Background

It is widely believed that Wu Hsin was born during the Warring States Period (403-221 BCE), postdating the death of Confucius by more than one hundred years.

This was a period during which the ruling house of Zhou had lost much of its authority and power, and there was increasing violence between states. This situation birthed "the hundred schools", the flourishing of many schools of thought, each setting forth its own concepts of the prerequisites for a return to a state of harmony. The two most influential schools were that of Confucius and the followers of Mozi ("Master Mo"), the Mohists. The latter were critical of the elitist nature and extravagant behaviors of the traditional culture. The philosophical movement associated with the Daodejing also was emerging at this time. Wu Hsin's style of Daoist philosophy developed within the context defined by these three schools and appears to be most heavily influenced by that latter. In addition, it most clearly contains the seeds of what would become Ch'an Buddhism in China or Zen in Japan.

Wu Hsin was born in a village called Meng, in the state of Song. The Pu River in which Wu Hsin was said to have fished was in the state of Chen which had become a territory of Chu. We might say that Wu Hsin was situated in the borderlands between Chu and the central plains—the plains centered around the Yellow River which were the home of the Shang and Zhou cultures. Certainly, as one learns more about the culture of Chu, one senses deep resonances with the aesthetic sensibility of the Daoists, and with Wu Hsin's style in particular.

If the traditional dating is reliable, Wu Hsin would have been a contemporary of Mencius, but one is hard pressed to find any evidence that there was any communication between them. The philosopher Gao Ming, although not a Daoist, was a close friend and stories abound of their philosophical rivalries.

Wu Hsin's work was significant for Daoist religious practitioners who often took ideas and themes from it for their meditation practice, as an example, Sima Chengzhen's 'Treatise on Sitting and Forgetting' (ca. 660 C.E.).

He offers a highly refined view of life and living. When he writes "Nothing appears as it seems", he challenges the reader to question and verify every belief and every assumption.

Brevity was the trademark of his writing style. Whereas his contemporaries were writing lengthy tomes, Wu Hsin's style reflected his sense that words, too, were impediments to the attainment of Understanding; that they were only pointers and nothing more. He would use many of the same words over and over because he felt that people needed to hear words repeatedly, until the Understanding was louder than the words.

His writings are filled with paradoxes, which cause the mind to slow down and, at times, to even stop. Reading Wu Hsin, one must ponder. However, it is not an active pondering, but a passive one, much in the same way as one puts something in the oven and lets it bake for a while.

He repeatedly returns to three key points. First, on the phenomenal plane, when one ceases to resist What-Is and becomes more in harmony with It, one attains a state of Ming, or clear seeing. Having arrived at this point, all action becomes wei wu wei, or action without action (non-forcing) and there is a working in harmony with What-Is to accomplish what is required.

Second, as the clear seeing deepens (what he refers to as the opening of the great gate), the understanding arises that there is no one doing anything and that there is only the One doing everything through the many and diverse objective phenomena which serve as Its instruments.

From this flows the third and last: the seemingly separate me is a misapprehension, created by the mind which divides everything into pseudo-subject (me) and object (the world outside of this me). This seeming two-ness (dva in Sanskrit, duo in Latin, dual in English), this feeling of being separate and apart, is the root cause of unhappiness.

The return to wholeness is nothing more than the end of this division. It is an apperception of the unity between the noumenal and the phenomenal in much the same way as there is a single unity between the sun and sunlight. Then, the pseudo-subject is finally seen as only another object while the true Subjectivity exists prior to the arising of both and is their source.

All five volumes consist of what would appear to be his day-to-day reflections as they spontaneously arose. There is no progression in the pages, no evolution of the concepts put forth. As such, reading pages randomly or from the beginning has the same efficacy. Nor should it be read with haste; a page or two at a time is sufficient to allow for the content to sink in, as a thrown stone falls to the bottom of the lake.

In its essence, this book is a collection of hooks; any one of them is sufficient to catch a thirsty fish

Translator's Note

Material of this nature is not served well by language. It may seem that there are anomalies and contradictions. So, it is important to state that the translation of Wu Hsin's words herein is not purely literal. Instead, it contains an interpretation of what was clearly implied, and this is where the limitation of words is quite evident.

Compounding this problem, I have chosen to incorporate certain words into the translation which may appear to be incongruent relative to the time of Wu Hsin's writing.

The clearest example of this would be my use of the word ego which wasn't to come into being for many of hundreds of years after Wu Hsin's death.

I have done this to best capture the real essence of the intention behind the word. The original Chinese word 个人 (ge ren) means the individual. However, using the individual doesn't capture the sense of separateness that is better conveyed by ego.

The Sanskrit language also provides us with some marvelous insight. In it, the word for mind is manas, which translated literally means that which measures and compares. That says it pretty well. The Sanskrit word for ego is ahamkara; its translation is *I am the doer*. Within the context of Wu Hsin's message, the conveyance of the idea of I am the doer is vitally important. As such, this and other small liberties that I have taken with the translation feel more than reasonable.

RM

In the Shadow of the Formless

Text

Using the flutist's flute
Does not make one
A flutist.
Wu Hsin has no tools,
No method to render.
He speaks of how it was for him,
Not implying that it will be
Likewise for another.

*****

Wu Hsin has no intended outcome in
The offering of these words,
Just as water is unconcerned
Whether or not
It quenches thirst.

*****

All individuals die.
Only those
Who are no longer individuals
Live forever.

One inherent error is
The preference for
The song of the future over
The seeming blandness of
The present moment.
Another error is
Using the mind
To try to understand
The words of Wu Hsin.
The mind is a tool
Unsuited to this task.
The proper tool is silence.
The seed is in the ground;
The sun will shine;
The rain will fall;
Nothing need be done.

*****

You believe that
There is nothing more than
Your God.
Wu Hsin says
There is nothing more than
Your God and
I am that Nothing.

*****

The reconciliation of
The feeling of separateness with
The reality of unity is
The enlightened view.
That which provided
The feeling of separateness
Takes it away.
There is nothing to be done.

What is derived from effort
Relates to the physical realm only.
What is derived from effortlessness, is
True knowing.
Not a knowledge of things, but
A knowing of What-Is.
Just as a spider
Spins a web out from itself,
So does each man spin his world
Out from himself.
Seeing this is
The beginning of the end.

*****

Everywhere one looks,
One sees aspects of
A single unity.
How can the seer, therefore,
Believe itself to be separate?
Is not the one who sees
Merely another aspect of
That which is seen?

*****

Although feeling lost is an illusion,
It is the first step in
Finding That which can
Never be lost.
Being is the seed of manifestation in which
All actions happen.
Just as a forest of trees is
Contained in a single seed,
So all of life is in
The seed of being.
Who, therefore, is doing anything?

Different instruments produce
Different sounds constituting
The melody of life.
The incense stick is lit.
It burns until
It is completely finished.
What remains is
The lighter of the stick.
He who sees the stick in himself and
Understands what Wu Hsin has said,
Has done very well.

*****

Thoughts are like
The promises of politicians and
Should be treated accordingly.
What is this body but
An animated corpse?
The investigation of the animator
Yields the knowing of which
Wu Hsin speaks.

*****

The music is latent in
The flute just as
The child is latent in
The mother.
See that you have
Brought your world with you.
Then, let it go.

*****

Giving attention to What-Is and
Not giving attention to
What appears to be, is
The key to opening
The prison door.

There may be many receptacles that
Hold the river water.
Yet, the quality of the water
Remains unchanged.
To identify with the receptacle is
The only error.

*****

All seeking is for
The cessation of pain.
When the seeker is gone,
The pain is gone.

*****

Trace your good luck
Back to its source or
Trace your bad luck
Back to its source and
You will discover that
The Source is the same.
From the One
Comes the Many.
As a baby nurses at
Its mother's breast,
One must nurse at
The source of life's sustenance
So that one may discover
The essence of being.

Being natural is
Being sacred.
Movement away from there is
Movement toward unhappiness.
The position is quite simple:
The One manifests as
The Many.
The water taken from the river is of
The same quality as
The water in the river although
It may appear in
A different vessel.

*****

If one sees oneself as
The center of everything with
The power to shape things
To suit one's desires, then
One has become
One's god.

*****

A dog does not know
He is a dog.
He only knows
He is.
If only man
Could be so fortunate.

Identification with a body is
The birth of the person,
The individual.
The personality then acts
To protect the body from
That which is
Other than itself.
When this false identification is
Seen through,
That which one truly is
Manifests and shines.

*****

Deep understanding,
True understanding is permanent.
The pickle never
Returns to being a cucumber.

*****

Until the boundary between
Inner and outer dissolves,
All changes are only minor.

*****

In the cessation of duality,
Oneness is revealed.
There can be no
Being one with…………
There is only being.

In ancient times,
Before there were individuals,
There were no problems.
Then, the individuals
Turned this against that and
Problems arose.
Identification with a body is
Merely a habit,
Taught to the child
Early in its life.
Breaking this habit is like
A chick breaking its shell.
What a wondrous world awaits.

*****

To depart from a vast no-thing
To become a small some-thing is
The pinnacle of foolishness.
Living spontaneously leaves
No time to think.
This is true living.

Choice is an illusion.
The individual having choice or
Not having choice is
Also an illusion.
What is an illusion?
It is when things are not
As they seem.
Once a realignment occurs,
One watches
What is happening
Without believing that
One is making it happen.
The body does what it chooses;
It wakes without permission,
Gets ill without permission.
Dies without permission.
All of this is to say,
A role is played;
Nothing more.

*****

Those who have re-cognized
Their true condition
Welcome whatever comes, thereby
Living life to its fullest.
The person is
A phenomenon in time.
Being is eternal.

Devotion to a teacher is
Far less important than
Devotion to a teaching.
True stillness,
Stillness without someone
Trying to be still, is
The solvent in which
All individual conditioning
Can be dissolved.
What remains is a neutrality,
An acceptance of What-Is.

*****

That which is often
Referred to as Emptiness
Could as easily be
Referred to as Fullness
Insofar as it contains
The potential for every thing.
Problems no longer appear
When the maker of the problems is
No longer part of the process.
That is to say that
The solution to all problems is
The removal of
The creator of all problems.

*****

How many eyes are required to
See the appearance of Being?
To change the world
One need only change
The color of the glass
One looks through.

All there is is
This manifestation and
Its perception.
This is the soup with
All the water boiled off.
Any identification with objects
Cuts off access to subjectivity, that is,
To the perceiving of
The wholeness that is inherent.

*****

Life is its own purpose.
That which perceives
Perceives the totality and the void.
This perceiving is prior to both.

*****

Wu Hsin is but an appearance;
Appearing to speak,
Appearing to convey concepts.
In fact, this here is
Only an object.
One in a world of objects.
It is through this object that
What-is is made known.
There is no specific way that
Things are supposed to be.
Something may be right one day and
Wrong the next.
Seeing things as they are,
Without judging,
Without labeling, is
A quality of those
Who live naturally.

Before there is a clear understanding,
When the bell above the door rings,
One opens the door.
After the clear understanding,
When the bell rings,
The door is opened.
The tyranny of the personal is that
It robs one of
The glory of being.
Confined to its cage,
The canary can never fly,
It can never soar.

*****

What is life other than
The Absolute functioning
Through Its instruments,
Resulting in this, which in turn,
Results in that.
In this fashion,
The web of causation is spun.
What happens after death?
The answer is simple:
The foreground no longer
Intercedes with the background.
Although not truly a return,
It is a return to that condition
Prior to birth.

*****

The body is here to do
What its nature requires.
It has nothing to do with
Anyone in particular.
When all intention is abandoned
What remains is silent awareness
Out of which emanates
Spontaneous living.

The fixation on objects, of which
Thought is one of many, is
The sole impediment to
Perceiving What-is.
Those who realize this are
No longer the body's accomplice.
A full bowl can have
No further utility.
Only when it is emptied,
Can it be put to use.
The Great Harmony is
Preceded by the emptying.

*****

To the blind,
The world is darkness.
To the deaf,
The world is silence.
The world is therefore
What the senses make it.
In turn,
What is sensed is
Filtered by the mind and, as such, is
What the mind interprets.

*****

The self-perpetuating mechanism
Referenced as the individual is merely
An artifact of memory.
It is like a top
That spins from its own inertia.

Do not seek progress as
Progress exists only in time.
The goal stands
Outside of time.
Believing in an independent entity is like
Believing that the wind
Blows the air.
The air is blown;
The blower cannot be found.

*****

Who is Wu Hsin other than
A bronze mirror in which
To see oneself clearly?
One cannot see
The whole world by
Looking through
A hole in the door.
Attaching certitude to
A limited view
Perpetuates all misconception.

*****

One's lamp may be
Different from Wu Hsin's lamp,
But the light is the same.
In naming,
The namer and the named
Become separate.
This is the beginning of the confusion.

Through the filter of
The personal
One can never see things
The way they are.
One can only see things
The way one is.
One may dwell on these matters for decades, but
Until insight triumphs over thought,
No lasting change can occur.
In the search for the Ultimate,
The intellect is as useless as
A lamp at noon.

*****

Being is irrefutable;
None can make the claim
I am not.
Do not remain
A prisoner of imagination and hearsay.
Inquire into
The validity of your beliefs and
Realize the foundation of all things.

*****

The separate self is
Only a function,
Similar in this regard to digestion.
Wu Hsin asks:
Why identify with it and
Live as a fraction of fullness instead of
Fullness itself?

*****

What is true can shine only
Once what is false
Has been disrobed.

A thorough examination of
One's assumptions and beliefs is
All that is required to see that
There is no map for
The way things are
Supposed to be.

*****

Awareness is
The Source of the world.
In its absence,
Who is aware of what?
Objects are dependent upon this awareness
For their existence.
Awareness depends on nothing.
It is self-sustaining, primal and
The underlying foundation of all things.
The quality of knowing to which
Wu Hsin speaks is demonstrated by
The answer to the question
Are you alive?
No thought,
No thinker is required.
The response is spontaneous.

*****

What one is
Is without direction.
Therefore, all going
Takes one away from it.
In the absence of all movement,
In stillness,
It arises of its own.
Where is the world
In the absence of
That which observes it?

The light of the fire
Casts shapes and shadows
Onto the wall.
It is the fascination
With the images that
Causes the forgetting of
The wall that supports them.
The face and
Its expression
Are not separate,
Are not two.

*****

Once the timeless perfection is seen
For what it is,
What can one want to add?
What can one want to take away?
That of which Wu Hsin speaks is not
An altered state.
It is the natural condition.
What most people perceive is
An altered state.

To become re-established in the natural,
May bring about a profound change or
It may be as subtle as
A knowing that one knows that
Something is different.
Wu Hsin cannot say
What to look for or
Where to look as
This naturalness cannot be
Named nor localized.
Solitude is a reflection of
The condition of the mind.
One can be in the forest,
Yet it can be said that
One is not in solitude or
One can be in the busy market and
Be in complete solitude.

*****

One's Source is not
External to oneself.
It is the foundation upon which
The notion of one's self is constructed.
Tear down the structure and
The foundation remains.
To find the I
Within every my, is
The key that unlocks
The Great Gate of Understanding.

The power of the will alone cannot
Bring one to the goal.
Only the One Who
Brought you to here can
Take you to there.
Being a person is
Only an idea.
It serves to mask
The underlying essence
In the same way that
Clouds obscure the sun.
When this idea is seen through,
What remains is brilliance itself.

*****

Living is the reaction to stimuli, to
People, events, and thoughts.
To examine the reactor is to
Inquire deeply into
The root of being.
That which contains the mind
Cannot be known
Via the mind.
In pristine silence,
This primal lucidity makes itself known.

Wu Hsin has no desire
To instill either fear or hope.
Instead, the sole purpose is to
Portray matters as they are, and
Thereby provide the ultimate freedom,
The freedom from concepts.
In order for understanding to flower,
One must forget everything,
Ceasing to set one thing
Against another.
Becoming an empty slate upon which
Writing appears and disappears.

*****

All problems are created by the mind and
Related to the body.
In the absence of either,
Where are the problems?

*****

Everyone is a single thought away from clarity.
Drop that thought and
See what remains.

The end of the tyranny
Created by the false sense of
A center controlling all that
Appears to happen is
Like a sun-filled dawn following
Weeks of rain.
One must not forget that
Wu Hsin's words are mere pointers
To something greater, and not
The Greatness Itself.
Just as one cannot drink
The word water,
One must not substitute these words for
The direct experience of What-Is.

*****

Pei owned a bird that
He wanted to set free.
He opened its door but
The bird did not move.
Wu Hsin told Pei:
A caged bird is not freed merely by
Opening the door.
Until the fear of the unknown subsides,
Until the desire arises
To fly away,
The bird remains where it is,
Preferring the known
To the unknown.

Taking away,
Taking away.
When everything has been
Taken away,
What remains is
The Ground that supports
The totality.
Seeing the Ground is
Being the Ground.

*****

Man is ensnared by
What he does no clearly see.
He becomes like the waterwheel,
Spinning, turning,
Purely mechanical.
See yourself as that in which
Worlds arise and set.
You are the unmovable background in which
All movement is perceived,
The weaver of all tapestries.
What can exist without you?
Answer this and
All other questions are finished.

*****

That which is false
Cannot withstand
The light of investigation.
The examination of
One's most central belief,
The existence of an acting me , is
The portal beyond.

This life is like
The wind;
One cannot know it directly.
It can only be known
Through its expressions.

*****

While Wu Hsin has grown older,
While his body has changed,
Presence remained unaltered throughout.
To take the changeful
For the changeless, is
The primary delusion.

*****

To be fully accepting of
What-Is in every moment,
Eliminates fear and anxiety,
Expectation and desire.
This is the natural way to
Set all things right.

Once there is the apperception that
One is but an instrument of
The Source of all things,
One can do what one pleases and
Live in whatever manner one chooses.
To relinquish the focus on
I was, and
The focus on I will be and
To remain fixed on I am,
The very seat of being,
The fundamental presence, is to
Return to the beginning,
To the Seed of Life
That one has never truly been left.

*****

Digestion is a process.
Thinking is a process.
Just as there is no digester, likewise
There is no thinker.
Thoughts appear.
Inquire onto what
Do they appear.
Being, expressed through the mind, is
I am.
This is the undeniable root.
Anything added to I am is
A movement away from It.

To understand that
One's true nature is
Imperceivable and inconceivable, is
The deepest understanding.
One who achieves this
Does not seek the good nor
Shun the evil.
What comes, comes; and
Sees clearly that, in time,
Everything comes.
There is no one choosing to hear.
There is no one choosing to smell.
There is no one choosing to think.
There is no one choosing to choose.

*****

Yanming Wei at last found peace.
There was nothing
He was attached to,
Nothing he was detached from.
He lost his opinions and
Found his way.

Cognition is prior to
Recognition.
The former arises in Being,
The latter is personal,
Arising from the mind as memory.
Whereas cognition is pure,
Recognition is tainted by
The supposed self-centre.
The world cognized is
A beautiful, wondrous world.
The world recognized is
Filled with alternating joy and sorrow.
It is not the mind that
Comes to this understanding.
It is the knower of the mind
Who knows this.
The moon's eclipsing of the sun
Never negates the existence of the sun.
It merely masks it.
Likewise, the personal eclipses
The divinity that
Resides in every man.
Its presence is felt in
The absence of
The seeming separate self.

Relinquish everything
That has been acquired and
Return to that state that existed
Prior to the first acquisition.
Now, tell Wu Hsin:
Who are you?
In the single instant,
Absent any thought,
There is the clear revelation that
Nothing is wrong.
The return of thoughts herald
The return of problems.

*****

Nature and its natural functioning are
The beginning and the end of all things:
Creation, Sustenance and Cessation.
The me is merely a distortion;
A personalizing of the impersonal.
When one discovers the truth of this,
All stories and dramas then
Become empty of meaning.
The past is dead, yet
The memory of the past
Lives on in
Someone with a past.

*****

Ultimately, the liberation of which
Wu Hsin speaks is the understanding that
One is not a spectator in the audience
Watching the actors perform.
One is a part of the play.
In so doing,
The notions of inside and outside are
Transformed into a single totality.

To some, the words of Wu Hsin are like
A spark in a container of cotton.
Others are wet cotton;
The spark has no effect.
Neither Wu Hsin nor
The spark nor
The cotton can be faulted;
What-is, is.

*****

Going out precedes returning.
When one has had
Their fill of the world,
One turns away and
Begins the return to
The abode that they never left.

*****

To live in unity,
There cannot be any one who is
Separate from any other.
All else is deception.

*****

For your search in this darkness,
Not even Wu Hsin can be one's lamp.
One must shine one's own light
On every belief
To come to the truth.

In the beginning,
There was Potential.
When the Potential,
By its very nature,
Becomes the actual,
Space is born.
Time is born.
Duality is born.
The world is born.
One is born.
This is the crux of
Unitive understanding.
To be open to discover this,
One must relinquish
One's death-grip on
All mental possessions.
Each being is
Moving toward the intended outcome of
Their inherent nature.
There is action
But no actor.

*****

There is no greater misfortune than
Misunderstanding.
To perceive That which makes the tongue speak but
Cannot be spoken by the tongue, is
The great good luck.
There is no greater fortune than
Understanding.

Fear is the attempt
To control the present moment.
When it becomes clear that
There are no others to fear,
Fear dissolves.

*****

With perfect insight that
Time is only the relegation of
Objective experience to
Past, present, and future; to
Recollection, consciousness, and anticipation,
One lives naturally,
Reacting spontaneously and appropriately
To every calling.
What is the mind
But a succession of thoughts,
Like beads on a string?
Deep understanding of
The workings of the mind is
The cutting of the string.
To understand that the mind is
The great divider,
Dividing function, seeing, into
Seer and seen, is
A great leap forward.

*****

When the confusion between
Beliefs and the actual is reconciled,
The world is seen in a new light.
The sole function of the mind is
To change, to alter, to modify
What-Is.
To reside prior to mind is
To reside in What-Is.

The way of Wu Hsin is
Through yourself to
Beyond yourself.

*****

-
Don't tell Wu Hsin
What you have relinquished.
It doesn't matter.
All that matters is
What you continue to
Hold on to.

*****

Wu Hsin claims nothing as
His own.
When one understands oneself to be
The ground from which
All things grow,
When there is no separate I,
How can there be any mine?

*****

Functioning comes before thought.
Seeing precedes I see
In the same way that
Being precedes identity.
To focus on the latter
At the expense of the former is to
Miss the mark.

Being-Awareness is every where
It is every when and
It is every thing.
All else is overlay.
The removal of the unnecessary
Allows what is primal to shine.
Dark clouds, mist and thunder
Have no effect on
The sun.
Seeing that you are That is
True freedom.

*****

They live in this present moment,
In the absence of the past.
Lacking a past,
They lack personality;
For what is personality but
A reaction to the past in the present?
Yet, in the absence of personality,
Can these be called persons?
Thoughts, feelings and perceptions may
Spontaneously appear.
Then, they subside.
Claiming ownership of them is the error.
Allowing them to arise and set without
Making them one's own is
The portal to peace.

*****

The solution cannot be
Found in time.
How much time is required to be
What one already is?

Sometimes, the shortest distance between two points
Runs through hell.

*****

Wisdom is the meeting of What-Is
With the same passion as
One's entertainment of what should be and
What shouldn't be.

*****

A cessation of confusion,
Equating different with separate,
Takes one to clarity.

*****

Everyone is aware but
Only the wise are
Aware of being aware.
To these, thinking and digestion
Function in the same manner,
Without attention or interest.

*****

Inside the bucket,
There is space.
Inside space,
There is the bucket.
Where then, is outer?
Where then, is inner?

Reality for the individual is
Made up of context, not content.
The characters on the scroll
Have different meanings to
Different readers.
The fire that is
Bad for the forest dweller
May be good for the forest.

*****

What-Is is needless as
It already contains everything.
The mind cannot know any thing
Any more than the ear
Can know the heard.

*****

Of all the renunciations,
Renunciation of the belief in
A separate, doing-self is the highest.
The common man seeks to
Straighten crooked trees and
Aid the growth of shorter ones.
The wise sees all the trees and
Fully accepts each as it is.

To remove a diseased tree from the soil,
One does not attack the branches
Nor the leaves.
One goes directly to the root.
To remove the spell of individuality,
Wu Hsin attacks the root of it.
In the end, it is revealed that
All seekers seeking are merely
Shadow boxing.
Simply be.
Within pure being,
All the actions that are necessary
Already reside.
They arise naturally and spontaneously,
Unaided by any one.

*****

From within the cage of imagination,
False views arise.
When seen as false,
These views dissipate,
Leaving only pristine clarity in their place.
Life makes one conscious,
Wu Hsin makes one aware.

*****

Those who seek
To control events
Can never be liberated from
Bondage to events.
To know that one is, is natural.
To know what one is,
Requires thorough investigation.

Whatever comes,
Must go.
What-Is is permanent,
Beyond all comings and goings.
Whereas you are focused on the structure,
Wu Hsin is concerned
Solely with the foundation.
Whereas structures rise and fall,
Foundations remain.
Whereas all experience is transient,
The ground of experience is
Immovable and permanent.

*****

To be what one is
Requires no practice.
The mind cannot discern
What is beyond the mind.
However, what is beyond the mind
Knows the mind intimately and
Supports it in the same way as
Silence is the support of all sound.

*****

Wu Hsin's advice is simple:
Let there be nothing that
You want to know;
What you need to know,
You'll come to know.
What is common to every experience is
Awareness of the experience.
You are That.
The rest is imagination.

There is a belief of separateness,
That you are separate from the rest.
There is nothing you can do
To rid yourself of this belief because
"You" is the belief.

*****

Understand fear to be
Estrangement from the Source.
Understand desire to be
Longing for the Source.
One can then see how
Returning to the Source is
The elimination of fear and
The satisfaction of desire.
And what is returning to the Source?
It is the recognition that
One is the sun and not
The clouds that obscure it.

*****

Phenomena are merely phenomena.
They arise and set continuously.
Labeling a phenomenon "me" is
The root problem.
When the attention is turned to
That which is primal,
All imaginations lose their hold.
What remains is pristine,
Unstained and ever-present.
Wu Hsin calls this Home.

One truly does not know
What one is and therefore
Takes oneself to be
What one is not.
The end of imagination is
The end of illusion.
The core of being
Requires no effort.
What is there
That must be done to
Be aware?

*****

One is nothing that
One is conscious of.
Yet one creates it all.
When the structure is dismantled,
The foundation is revealed.
Wu Hsin can point to the sky;
The seeing of the stars is
One's own.

*****

Great effort is required to see that
Clear sight is not
The result of effort.
Overlooking what is obvious is
The common obstacle.
To see what has been
Shining in plain view is
The simple remedy.

So much time spent,
Seeking what one is.
So much better is it to understand
What one is not.
Then what remains is pure and
What one is.

*****

Movement is inherent in
The very nature of the mind.
That is to say,
Thoughts appear.
To believe that
One can stop thought is
Tantamount to believing that
One can make a tiger bleat.

*****

Correct one's jaundiced eye and
Nothing will appear to be yellow.
The I in "I think" is as real as
The it in "it rains".

*****

How can it be that
So many would choose
The doorway to
A public discourse on heaven over
The doorway to heaven?
Separating oneself from
One's beliefs
Results in the ending of the beliefs and
An ending of the separate self.

Clear seeing is
Understanding that one is not
A fragment of the whole;
Nothing more and
Nothing less.
Once freed from all opposing pairs
Such as good and bad,
Desirable and undesirable,
What one does
Can never be wrong.

*****

The body, the mind and the intellect
All grow, become mature and decay.
However, That which sees this
Remains unmoved,
As it ever was.
One can easily see
Oneself in the world.
But only those who can see
The world in oneself are truly free.

*****

To be what one is
Requires no effort.
One is present,
One is aware,
Therefore, one is.
No authority,
No teacher,
Can give one
What one already is.

Taking an illusion to be real is delusion.
Recognizing an illusion
As an illusion does not
Dissipate the illusion.
It dissipates delusion.
This is lucidity.

*****

There is never enough time
In the present moment
To have a thought about
The present moment.

*****

Difference does not mean separation.
Fingers may appear different, but
They are not separate from
The hand, which is not separate from
The body.
When all is seen as
A single, coherent unity,
Fear must dissolve because
There is nothing
Apart from oneself to fear.

*****

The only thing that is
More difficult than
Looking for a grain of rice in
A pile of straw is
Looking in the wrong pile.
Where are you looking for
What you are seeking?
If it is outside yourself, you are
Looking in the wrong pile.

The actual arises from
The potential;
The manifest arises from
The Unmanifest and,
In its appropriate time,
Returns to It.
Mortals call this Life.

*****

It is correct to say
I am nowhere.
Likewise, it is correct to say
I am now here.

*****

To arrive at the taste of the mouth,
Requires the elimination of
All tastes in the mouth.
Likewise, to know what one is
Requires the elimination of
All that one is not.

*****

The Cave may have been dark
For ten thousand years.
No matter.
Shine a torch inside it and
All darkness disappears.

*****

The mind cannot be
The arbiter of
That which is
Beyond its jurisdiction.

One need not wait
To become
What one already is.

*****

From the unified view,
There is nothing that is mine,
Just as there is nothing that is
Not mine.

*****

The more one thinks about
What-Is,
The more one veils
What-Is.

*****

They come and ask Wu Hsin
What to do.
What is to be done?
By whom?
Being the very heart of Being
Can be the only reply.

*****

The individual desires liberation.
But, liberation from what?
Liberation from the pain of
Being an individual.
Can you not see why
Wu Hsin laughs so hard?

A central misunderstanding of
Those who visit Wu Hsin is that
They believe that
There is something to attain to.
How can one attain to
What one already is?

*****

Confusion is a mental state based on
Viewing events through the lens of
Unexamined assumptions.

*****

What can be simpler
To understand than this?
One lives in the house, but
One is not the house.

*****

Everything ultimately returns to
The Infinite.
Water evaporates,
A body dies;
There is no difference.

*****

To live naturally,
To be in that Natural state,
Requires no effort.
Effort is only required
To be something in particular.

All practices are performed by
The individual.
When the individual is
Understood to be a shadow,
Not a separate and distinct entity,
The need for practices drops off.
Investigate the reality of the shadow and
It must disappear.

*****

The fear of death is
The penalty for accepting
The idea of individuality.
When the particular is seen to be
No different than the universal
The fear of death is gone.

*****

Pang Yi stared out across
The expanse of the blue ocean.
He decided he wanted to
Have some for himself; so
He went to the shoreline with his bucket.
Yet, regardless of his efforts
No blue water went into his bucket.
Man lives with illusions.
Knowing illusions to be illusions is
The way out of illusion.

*****

The heart beats.
The body excretes.
Thoughts come.
Thoughts go.
All there is
Is the functioning.
All else is story.

Do not become
More enamored with the path
Than with the goal.

*****

To believe that Wu Hsin has
Something to give is an error.
To believe that one
Needs to get something is
Yet another error.
There is nothing to be given
Nor anything to be gotten.

*****

Seeing illusion as illusion
Does not dissolve the illusion,
Only its power.

*****

Although clouds may appear,
The sun is not fazed.
They come and they go;
The sun remains.
My child, you are the sun itself.

*****

Immortality, that is,
Eternal life, can only be realized
Through daily death.
In so doing,
That which cannot die is revealed.

The desire to
Acquire some esoteric knowledge
Can hold great power.
But esoteric knowledge will never
Take one to the place that is
The support of all knowledge.
Such support does not
Reside in the unknown.
Rather, it resides in the unknowable.

*****

Never allow concepts to
Substitute for direct insight.

*****

When no energy is directed toward
Perpetuating a story about an individual
The individual vanishes.

*****

What school must one attend to
Learn how to be oneself?

*****

My dear, what you are looking for is
Right in front of your eyes.
What you are looking for is likewise
Behind your eyes.

All supposed problems are of the mind.
What is mind?
Mind is the collection of thoughts.
Where are the problems when
They are not thought about?

*****

All manifestation is in
The realm of the opposites:
Good and bad,
Hot and cold,
Beautiful and ugly.
Before these arise is
One's natural Home.

*****

The image in the mirror may
Appear to have a life of its own.
This is only an illusion.
In the mirror of pure awareness,
Forms may appear to have lives of their own.
This, too, is an illusion.

*****

Lao Bing tried to
Drive his fencepost into the ground with
The use of his whip.
Wrong tool!
Do not use the mind to
Comprehend the words of Wu Hsin.
Wrong tool!

There is only pure functioning;
There is no functioner.
The heart beats;
There is no beater.
The lungs breathe;
There is no breather.
Seeing this clearly is emancipation.

*****

Fruit does not ripen itself.
Therefore, what is there to be done?

*****

Although there is seeing,
That which sees
Cannot be seen.
Wu Hsin calls this
The Great Mystery.

*****

Why bemoan what one was,
What one might have been,
While ignoring what one is
In every moment?
Is this not
The heart of unhappiness?

*****

When thought is stopped,
Being goes on.
Thoughts come,
Thoughts go.
Being, the root,
Does not move.
You are That.

Ruthless examination of one's assumptions
About oneself,
About who one is,
About what one is,
Removes all the falsehoods that
Undermine clear sight.
What remains is what had been
Overlooked from the beginning.

*****

Oneness has no reference point,
No center.
What is it that can
Stand outside of everything?

*****

Understanding is everything.
When the cause of the problem falls away,
The effects of the problem do likewise.

*****

Why visit Wu Hsin when
What is sought is within?

*****

Winter never wishes
It was summer.
Remove all resistance to What-Is.
This is completion.

Light is there,
Darkness is there.
What holds them?
In what do they reside?
The solution to this mystery is
The solution to your own mystery.

*****

A thought appears, lingers and then disappears.
Where did it come from?
Where does it go?
There is a birth, a life, and then a death.
Where did it come from?
Where does it go?

*****

The only salvation that one needs is
The salvation from one's own imagination.

*****

The personal is
Merely an appearance.
What the person perceives is
Also an appearance.
The perceived and the perceiver are
Not separate;
They are the flavor of perception.

*****

There is a primal
Source of light by which
Everything is seen.
Those who have understood, know that
They are That.

The sound of the gong
Fills the entire space of the room.
In the same manner,
Consciousness fills
The entire space of space.

*****

You come before
Anything that can be observed.
Discern this fully and
The world cannot hold you.

*****

Experiences can be described in
Thousands of ways.
But, who is it that can
Describe the Experiencer?

Lan Xi sought wisdom.
His first teacher taught him
"You are the screen on which all appears and disappears".
Lan Xi was not satisfied.
His second teacher taught him
"You are the screen on which all appears and disappears".
Lan Xi was not satisfied.
His third teacher said,
"First you must serve me for ten years.
Only then will I teach you"
And so it was that
For ten years, Lan Xi served the teacher,
Cleaning the dung from the animal stalls,
Sweeping the floors,
Cooking the meals and
Washing the clothes.
At the conclusion of the ten years, Lan Xi said:
"I have fulfilled my commitment and
I am now ready to receive your teaching".
"Very well" said the teacher.
"You are the screen on which all appears and disappears".

*****

What substance can a belief have
Once its falseness is seen through?
Once all the falseness is seen through,
What remains is What-Is.

When the light of consciousness is
Cast onto that which is called life,
It creates a shadow that
Runs parallel to life.
This shadow is the thought I-am.
The movement of life is
Therefore shadowed by
The movement of thought.
One must not forget that
That which runs parallel can never
Touch that to which it runs parallel.

*****

The mind caught up in seeking
Misses what is obvious.
The vastness in front of one's eyes is
No different than the vastness
Behind one's eyes.

*****

Every thing is simply
Primal energy
Appearing in a form.
You are no different.
Seeing this clearly
Nothing is right or wrong.

*****

The known may come and go, while
Knowing remains, unchanging.
Thoughts appear on this Knowing.
The concept of a thinker is
Added afterwards.

One cannot carry any scripture through
The doorway of liberation.

*****

Make no distinction between
The awareness of presence and
The presence of awareness.
There is none.

*****

The word is not the thing.
One can't drink the word water.
Exercise extreme caution not to
Confuse one for the other.

*****

How many more years can you
Ignore what is basic and
Remain preoccupied with this passing show?

*****

The salt is
Already in the sea water.
The core of what the individual is,
Is in place before the individual arrives.
That which is impersonal
Appears as the personal.
The central fixation
Must be dropped:
There is no individual.

"I am" is a translation of
The sense of pure being.
It is distorted when
It becomes personal.

*****

One cannot stand solidly on
One's own feet until
One's crutches are discarded.

*****

How can the indescribable be described?
Wu Hsin can only say that
The Knower of Being comes first;
All else follows from That.

*****

The disease is a simple one to diagnose;
Its primary symptom is
The continuous belief in the erroneous.

*****

It is only
The sense of a separate me
That is born.
The dissolution of this sense is
Its very death.
One need not die
To achieve this.

Life pulsates.
Everything is happening but
There is no one to
Whom it is happening.

*****

What-Is is.
It has always been.
It will always be.
There is nothing that
Needs to be done.
There is no place to go.
There is nothing to get.
Clarity is not about adding;
It is about taking away.

*****

Rainwater flows through
Old pathways in the soil.
It is nature's habit.
Believing in a doer-entity is
Merely another habit.

*****

Reading the calligraphy,
One forgets the parchment
On which it is written.
The parchment is prior to the writing.
A subtle shift in perception
Brings the parchment to the foreground.
Then, everything is clear.

Seeking the extraordinary,
It is easy to overlook
The ordinary.
Yet, that which is ordinary is
The foundation and support of all things.

*****

The present instant,
Now,
Resides outside of time.
It is not quantifiable.
It cannot be measured.
It cannot be grasped.
It is the meeting place of
All events.

*****

One who identifies
With the body,
Dies with the body.
One who does not, is
Immortal.
For such a one,
There is no rebirth because
There has been no birth.

*****

The mirage of an egg cannot be
Shattered by any mallet.
Likewise, the mirage of a separate self
Cannot be shattered by any individual.
The individual is, itself,
The mirage.

Peace and stillness are found at
The center of the vortex.
One receives the product of
Where one resides.
Do not live in
A noisy neighborhood if
Quiet is desired.

*****

Thoughts are merely stories,
Stories about a "me" or about
An "other-than-me".
They come,
They go.
They are unimportant.
Seeing this,
The focus on content can be dropped,
Revealing the clear Being-Seeing-Knowing
That has been there all along.

*****

Because its wants are fewer,
A well cared for dog is always
Happier than its master.

*****

Wu Hsin has no prescription to
Make life filled with
More pleasure and less pain.
Life is the pulsating amalgam of both.
This cannot be changed.
To resist this is
To suffer needlessly.

Although thoughts appear in the present,
Their content is always about
The past or the future.
These are mere stories that
Serve to distract from
The knowing of What-Is.

*****

One's image of oneself is
Referred to as I or me.
But that is all it is,
An image.
It cannot plow the fields.
It cannot cook the rice.
What plows the fields,
What cooks the rice was
Before all I's and me's.
You are That.

*****

With the personal as
The reference point,
Life is viewed as if
Through a keyhole.
With the personal
Out of the way,
The fullness is clearly discerned.

Being is the great mystery.
It cannot be found since
It is no thing; yet,
It can be felt since
It is in every thing.
Presence is acknowledging
What is here,
Right now.
Being-Presence is directing the attention to
This very instant and
Not becoming distracted by thought.
Gaining mastery over thought
Does not eliminate thought.
It merely strips it of all of
Its hypnotic power.
Then, every moment is fresh and new.

*****

On can never get enough of
What does not satisfy.

*****

There are no situations
Separate from the Totality.
All situations are
Aspects of this Totality.
The view from the Totality is
Always different from
The situational view.

*****

Seekers of Oneness,
Ignoring the obvious:
Wu Hsin newly presents that which is
Infinitely ancient.
Be still and understand this.

Complete Understanding is comprised of
Both Understanding and
Living the Understanding.

*****

To trust in
What one thinks one knows
Leads one astray.
To trust in
The source of knowing is
The course to be taken.

*****

True freedom is
The absence of all agendas.

*****

There is only one error:
Giving attention to the content and
Ignoring the space that
Supports the content.
With a slight shift in viewpoint,
All is aligned.

*****

Wu Hsin will not give you
What you want.
Wu Hsin only gives
What you need.
Then, the mysteriousness leads you to
Where you must go.

The mind is an excellent tool
For identifying differences.
It is a poor tool
For identifying Oneness.
Why use a mallet when
The task requires an ax?

*****

So much more energy
Would be available if
It weren't squandered on
Maintaining a self image.
Over time, all these "myselfs"
Change, then disappear.
That which has never changed,
That which will never change, is
The fertile soil for exploration.

*****

All appearances are
Mere movements of energy in
The field of consciousness.
What one is, is
The knower of the field.

*****

Out of the fullness of emptiness,
Everything arises.
Everything returns.
Wise men understand this as
The play of life.

There is no need to
See,
Get,
Realize or
Find out any so-called truth.
Must one see,
Get,
Realize or
Find out that one is?
That one is, is
The primal truth.

*****

There is nothing to practice.
All practices are like
Painting a rose so that
It will smell better.

*****

Smoke may fill the sky, but
The sky remains unaffected.
Once it is recognized that
One is the sky,
Events in the sky
Lose their hold.
Wu Hsin is the wind that
Blows away the smoke.

*****

Fighting with the mind
Strengthens the mind.
Seeing through the mind to
What is prior to it,
Takes all its power from it.

Balance is always attained effortlessly.
Effort impedes that attainment of balance.
Wu Hsin advises:
Don't get in the way.

*****

One need not analyze darkness
In order to dispel it.
Light the lamp of clarity and
All darkness is dispelled.
If the question How arises,
One has not understood.

*****

The only difference between
A teacher and a student is that
The student believes that
There is a difference whereas
The teacher knows there is none.

*****

Right here,
Right now, is
All that there is.
Everything else is
A creation of the mind.

*****

Time cannot be used to
Find the timeless.

*****

The natural life is not
A life without warts.

Lao Wei came to Wu Hsin and said:
"Master, I have become a cat".
Wu Hsin replied "No, Lao Wei,
You are not a cat.
You are a human being"
Lao Wei then asked:
"Then how did I become a cat?"
There are always some
Who refuse to see.

*****

Giving up a little,
One gets a little.
Giving up a lot,
One gets a lot.
Giving up everything,
One gets everything.

*****

Those who possess true wisdom are transparent.
With nothing to protect,
With nothing to defend,
It is easy to see through them.

*****

When life is lived
Without distinctions,
Nothing can go wrong.

Amidst the totality,
There is infinite uniqueness.
Yet, nothing is separate.
Just as the finger is unique to the hand,
The hand unique to the arm,
The arm unique to the torso.
The torso unique to the body and
The body unique in the world,
So, too, all beings are unique within
One continuous wholeness.
The only "have-to" is that
One has to be.
Once established in being,
All else unfolds naturally and effortlessly.

*****

Nothing is to be gained by
The study of shadows.
To discern the substance
Underlying the shadow is wisdom.
The world appears simultaneously with
The one who sees it.
The former cannot be,
In the absence of the latter.

*****

Manifestation is named forms
Floating in empty space,
Observed through time.
Yet, the observer,
Residing on the outside,
Remains wrapped in mystery.

Ask yourself this:
Over the course of your life,
How many identities have
You created for yourself?
Where are they now?
How long do you believe that
Your present identity will last?
Where does it go when it is finished?

*****

Where is the boundary between the silence and
The peal of the temple gong ringing; or
Between the cresting wave and
The vast ocean?
All there is is
Arising and falling within
The Great Unity.

*****

The most efficient means to
Destroy any problem is to
Ignore the problem.
In the absence of the energy
Required to sustain it,
It withers and dies.

*****

As one cannot be taught
How to fall asleep,
One cannot be taught
How to awaken.
Slumber happens,
Awakening happens without
Any one doing any thing.

There is no chaos.
It is only thought that
So names it.
Prior to naming,
Prior to labeling,
Where is the problem?

*****

Conception and gestation is progressive
Whereas birth is sudden.
Likewise is the birth of understanding.

*****

Within the world of things,
One's true nature is as
The knower of all things, and
Not as a thing itself.
When all thoughts,
Emotions and
Sensations are set aside,
What remains is the Essence.

*****

The belief that Wu Hsin is special,
Perpetuates the hope that
One can also be special.
This, too, must go.

*****

All things appear as
They truly are to those
Who are not blinded by self interest.

How can one lose
What is infinite?
Where would it go?

*****

To know that
The mind is empty is good.
To know the knower of
The empty mind is better.

*****

Everyone is only a single thought
Away from perfection.

*****

There is breathing.
There is seeing.
There is functioning.
Where is the need
For a "me" to allow all that?

*****

Whatever can be gained
Can be lost.
What cannot be gained is
What is already present,
Here and now.
Realign with this and nothing else.

*****

Thinking imposes itself on silence as
Unwelcome relatives impose themselves on family.

The mind is the Great Divider,
Taking each from the Undivided to
The divided.
The mind cannot contain the Undivided.
The Undivided contains the mind.

*****

The world is the food that
Satisfies the hunger of feeling separate.
When the feeling is
Seen to be erroneous,
The hunger subsides and
The world loses its power.

*****

Pure attention attends.
It is the ability to perceive
What arises in every moment
Without reacting to it.

*****

Having no aspirations is
The gateway to freedom.
To relinquish control over
One's experiences,
To allow them to be
Just as they are, is
The invitation.

Using concepts as
One uses a net,
To capture ideas, can never
Produce the ultimate understanding.
To realize that which cannot be captured,
That which cannot be contained, is itself
The ultimate understanding.

*****

Those who come to Wu Hsin with
The desire to obtain something are
Sure to be disappointed.

*****

What is permanent within
The transient?
Finding this,
The seeking ends.
The seeker ends.

*****

The unexpected is
Bound to happen.
That which is anticipated
May never arrive.
Who is to say?
All is solely because
One is.

*****

For those who have apperceived,
All action is spontaneous,
Action without reaction.
Action without an actor.

The rain is falling.
The grass is growing.
The crows are calling.
Where is the effort in this?
The desire to arrive somewhere,
Of a destination for a "me"
Shackled to time,
Impedes the realization that
All there is is this singular moment.
Right here,
Right now.

*****

There is nothing to change.
The mind and the body
Continue to do
What they do.
The one who knows
The mind and the body is unmoved.

*****

The sense of being this or that is
The final outpost before
Arriving at Being Itself.
It is now time to
Leave this outpost behind.

*****

Yes,
This too.

As a young boy,
Wu Hsin would often travel in
The back of the oxcart.
In the heat of the afternoon,
He would often see
What appeared to be water on the roadway.
As he drew closer to it,
It vanished and
He therefore understood it
To be merely an illusion.
To this day, when traveling,
Wu Hsin still sees
The water on the road.
But knowing it to be an illusion,
It has no power and
Garners no attention.

*****

All attempts to change
This moment into something else,
Can only occur in the next moment.
Full acceptance of what
Appears in this moment is
The style of sages.

*****

If It cannot be found
Where one already is,
Where does one have to
Go to secure it?

*****

To liberate oneself from false notions,
False ideas and
False concepts,
Shatters the shackles that
Keep one small.

One is the space in which
The world appears.
There is nothing left to say.

*****

Wu Hsin is not dispensing recipes.
There is no cook.
There is only cooking.

*****

Breaking a habit begins by
Acknowledging the habit.
Until this occurs,
There can be no change.

*****

No matter how many things
Seem to be wrong,
There are many more that are right,
Just the way they are.
When nothing is ever wrong,
One joins
The company of the wise.

*****

Insights may arise.
Yet, no one,
No thing, makes them arise.
The arising is a spontaneous event.

In a room filled with objects,
There is more space,
More emptiness, than
There are objects.
This space is the support of everything and
To ignore it is
To ignore It.
One is that That,
That It, in which
Everything rises and sets.

*****

The knowing that
There is an Unknown that
Cannot be known, is
The dawn of wisdom.
To kiss this Unknown is
To be truly in love.

*****

When seeing is divided into
The seer and the seen,
What-Is is lost.

*****

Do not desire cloudless skies.
Clouds appear,
May stay for some time and
Then the clouds evaporate.
The sun holds no preferences.

The body is
The screen on which
All images,
All sensations,
Appear and disappear.
One is not the screen.
One is the Knowing of the screen.

*****

To believe that
Thoughts have power,
To believe that
Thoughts are true is the source of suffering.
The only power in thought is
The power one assigns to it.
True knowledge is not
Derived from thought.
It is derived from
The inner wellspring that one is.

*****

One is not a
Part of the whole.
One is
The Source of the whole.

*****

Second hand knowledge
Conveyed by a third person is
Hearsay only.
Throw away all the books,
All the stories, and
Return to the Essence
That has never gone anywhere.

There are no solutions
Out there.

*****

The caged bird won't fly away
Even if the door is open.
Wu Hsin can open
The door to your cage, but
There are no guarantees
Pertaining to a desired outcome.

*****

As the sky is
The unchanging context
For the weather.
Silent emptiness is the
Foundation of all things.

*****

To be perfect is
To see the Perfection.
It is this Perfection in which
The body, the mind and the world
Arise, linger and set.

*****

Once there is surrender to
Never finding out
Who one is,
Who one is becomes obvious.

Man's primary function is to
Create unhappiness for others.
This ceases when
It is understood that
There are no others.

*****

Everything happens at the same time.
That time has a name:
Suddenly.

*****

When the mind is not
Preoccupied with thought,
The transitory is no longer
The center of attention.
Then, a deeper intelligence takes over, and
Everything is exactly as it should be.

*****

Every thing is only energy,
Sometimes seemingly harmonious,
Sometimes seemingly disharmonious.
Those that know the energy are not
Concerned with harmony or disharmony or
Labels of any kind.

*****

As soon as an idea arises of
How it should be or
How it should have been or
How it will be,
The center is lost.

Can a man seek his own hands?
You are your own mountaintop.
All seeking is
A movement away from there.

*****

In seeing,
Both the seer and the seen are experienced.
Identification with the seer is
An error of the mind.

*****

What is clear and present cannot be
Observed by the senses.
It can only be pointed to.
Wu Hsin does nothing else.

*****

The world is known
Through the mind, but
The support of the world cannot be
Known through the mind because
It is prior to the mind.

*****

One's life is lived
Not by beliefs, but
By inner convictions.
This is the Knowing from which
Wu Hsin speaks.

All desires are lies in that
They promise a lasting payoff.
Desirelessness is the truth in that
There is nothing to be gained and
Nothing to be lost.

*****

It is only by
Removing all of the water-plants that
The full scope and majesty of
The water can be discerned.
The impediment is
The preoccupation with the plants.

*****

Those who are clear accept both
The diamonds in the necklace and
The garbage on the street.

*****

All sentient beings must see
Where the sentience has come from.
The Being-Sentience must be,
Before the appearance of sentient beings.
This is the original state.

*****

The sunlight hits the crystal and
Rainbows of color appear.
Yet, what difference can be found between
The sunlight and the rainbows?
Is the latter not the former?

When the desire to become
This or that is set aside,
Being flowers.
In that, what is revealed is
What one really is:
The watching of
What one believes oneself to be.
This is not an awakening for any me.
This is an awakening from any me.

*****

The known arises,
The unknown remains hidden, yet
Both are merely events
Occurring in the Unknowable.
This Unknowable can be given endless descriptions,
But it can never be seen.

*****

Everything is merely
Perceived.
It is only later that
The perceiver stakes his claim and
Labels, categorizes, and judges.
First there is existence and presence.
It is only later that
My existence and presence arrives.
Since one cannot be
What one perceives,
What is one really?

*****

All needs are provided through
The process of the natural functioning.
All wants are for and from the individual.
Wants are attended to by the functioning only
Insofar as they align with the functioning.

When clarity is present,
There are never problems.
When clarity is absent,
There are always problems.

*****

There is a single Source of every thing.
Happiness and sorrow do not
Arise from different places.
The location of this Source is
The Great Mystery.

*****

It is only a madman who
Searches for something that
He hasn't lost.
Where does one have to go
To find what is already here?

*****

Self consciousness creates the individual.
This self consciousness or I-thought
Births all separation.
Prior to self consciousness,
There is no individual.
There is no central point of reference.
There is only Being, Awareness, Presence.
This is the natural state,
One of integral perception.

*****

True understanding manifests with
The cessation of the question
What's in it for me?

Wu Hsin's lodestone always
Points in the same direction:
Here.

*****

The natural ones are momentary, transitory.
What they were,
They are not now.
What they will be
They are not now.
Against this ever-changing background,
They have no fixed center.
With no fixed center,
Nothing is personal.

*****

When everything is allowed
When everything is invited,
Without judgment or discrimination,
How can peace not prevail?

*****

When the smells from the kitchen
Overtake the awareness,
Reading the menu loses its appeal.
Likewise, one cannot learn to swim
While remaining dry.

Taking the mind
Upstream to its source,
Resolves confusion and
Clarifies what has been obscured.
It is here that I am is
Transformed into there is.

*****

The wise have abandoned all imaginings.
Imaginations of the past are gone.
Imaginations of the future are gone.
They are thrust into
The present moment where
Everything that has happened
Seeded what is happening.
They are now living without
A formula for living.

*****

That which registers all feelings,
That which registers all sensations,
That which registers all perceptions,
That which registers the entire content of the mind,
Wu Hsin names the Registrant, and
This is the true core of what one is.
It is no thing, and, as such
It cannot be known.
It can only be experienced by
No one in particular.
If you must ask Wu Hsin
"When will I know that I understand?"
Wu Hsin can only reply:
"Not yet".

Belief is a poor substitute for understanding.
To begin to question one's beliefs is to
Begin to understand.

*****

When both the acceptable and the unacceptable
Become acceptable,
Living is effortlessly easy.

*****

Seeing oneself to be
The knowing of all things and
The source of all things,
Upon which all things depend,
What is the further use of one's gods?

*****

There is nothing to become.

*****

Scrutinizing the moon
Reflected in the lake
Limits the understanding of
The moon in the heavens.

*****

Over the course of time,
The body changes.
The identities change,
The images of one's self changes.
Yet, something remains unchanged throughout it all.
It is mistakenly referred to as me;
Yet, it is not that.
It is That through which
All me's are known.

The end of the individual is not
The end of greatness.
It is the end of smallness.
Wu Hsin calls this
The Great Breaking.

*****

Thinking is the emphasis of
Content over process.
Consciousness is the emphasis of
Process over content.
Attention is the bridge between the two.

*****

Once the understanding is
Complete and clear,
There is nothing to do except
To watch.

*****

Being is one.
Ways of being are infinite.

*****

Only the wisest understand that
The word me is a verb and
Not a noun.
They no longer
Walk through life with
Eyes half opened and
Hearts half closed.

Do not chase experiences;
They come and they go, like
Shadows cast on the wall.
Instead, chase That which experiences.
Catch It and
One arrives at
The home one never left.

*****

Regardless of the number of voices,
They all emanate from
One tongue.

*****

Do not become enamored with
The words of Wu Hsin.
The value in
The words of Wu Hsin is that
They reveal the
Limitations of words.

*****

Wu Hsin does not recommend
Doing anything at all.
Wu Hsin does not recommend
Not doing anything at all.
Both are a movement away from
What-Is.

The light that
Looks through these eyes today
Is the same light that
Looked through them
Sixty years ago.
Understanding that one is that light is
The apperception of infinity.

*****

The observer spends a lifetime
In conflict with the observed.
This is resolved when
The observer is also the observed and
The two dissolve into the observing.

*****

That which is ever-present must be
Prior to all things that come and go.
Rigorous scrutiny reveals that
This is what one is.

*****

It is said that
Those with integral vision are
Filled with emptiness.
Those with dust in their eyes
Cannot see this.

Isn't it humorous that
People spend their entire lives
Trying to become a better story?
When the story is recognized to be
Just a story,
The energy directed toward
Maintaining the story dissipates.
Then, there is nothing that
Can be pointed to and claimed:
This is what I am.

*****

Eyes are not required for insight.

*****

All these dramas are like
The blowing of the wind.
In time, it ceases.
Outside of time, it never was.

*****

Those who are shining
Have no location in space.
Rather, space is located in them.

*****

Weeds have their place too.

*****

Being is the seed from which
All worlds,
All gods and
All forms sprout.
It parents every thing.

All problems are
Born in the mind and
Delegated to the body.
To see through this is to,
Realize one's true luminosity.

*****

Those with integral vision have
Cast off all definitions,
All labels, of
Who they are.
In truth, these only apply to
The body and its actions.
At the core, they are
That which cannot be defined.

*****

The only difference between
A silver coin and silver dust is in appearance.
In essence,
There is no difference.
Fools dwell on appearances
Whereas masters live in essence.

*****

The past is in memory.
The future is in imagination.
All that there is, is this instant.
Don't lose it to inattention.
Once it is gone,
It is gone.

Every action is a movement of energy.
The wave on the ocean is not
The movement of water.
It is the movement of
Energy through water,
The movement of
The Animator through the inanimate.
To see this clearly is to
Understand the workings of the universe.
When there is understanding of
The workings of the universe,
There can be no
Resistance or opposition.
When there is no
Resistance or opposition.
All that remains is peace.

*****

To have the courage to
Question one's certainties, is
True courage.

*****

How can we speak of a center
When the center is everywhere?

*****

Do not add Wu Hsin's words to
The catalogue of concepts.
Wu Hsin's words don't
Point to adding;
They point to taking away,
And taking away,
And taking away.

All thoughts are like
Smoke in the sky;
Here one minute,
Gone in the next.
Why assign importance to them?
Is the smoke important?

*****

The seeing happens before
The I see can be said.
The I see is merely
A skewed translation of
There is seeing.
All I's and me's are
Translations of the mind which
Skews the impersonal into
Something personal.

*****

There is no owner;
No one to claim:
My body or
My thoughts.
There is no owner of consciousness.
Consciousness owns everything.

*****

The unfoldment of the Infinite is
From I to I am to
I am this object in space and time.
The perceiving assumes the roles of
The perceiver and the perceived.
Nothing is added,
Nothing is taken away.

Only a wise one
Recognizes everything as a lie,
Including the recognizer.

*****

Just as the answer
Contains the question,
The student contains the teacher.

*****

There is no way out.
There is no way in.
No way is necessary.
To discover that which is
Outside of time,
Requires nothing bound by time.

*****

Those that are truly religious are
Untouched by the temples, the prayers,
The rites and the dogma because
They discern that what is truly religious is
Prior to all these and
This is where they come to rest.

*****

Chasing after transcendental experience is
Merely another escape.
When What-Is is fully embraced and accepted,
What needs to be added?

To empower the transitory is
To become its slave.
The seeing through the transitory is
Its mastery.

*****

As long as the mind is,
The body and the world are.
The support of all these is
Before all these.
The natural ones call this Home.

*****

One cannot suggest that
Sugar and sweetness are separate.
Nor can one suggest this regarding
Man and his god,
Regardless of how it may seem.

*****

From unitary wholeness,
What needs to be done,
Comes up to be done.
This is the natural functioning.
To believe that
There is some one
Doing something,
Obscures What-Is with
What seems to be.

*****

True wisdom dawns with
The rejection of conventional wisdom.

The Ultimate Ground of Being is not
Amenable to dissection.
While one may seek to
Explore the unknown,
One cannot know
The Unknowable.

*****

Where does Wu Hsin call Home?
He resides in the space between
The nothingness from which he emerged and
The infinity that envelops him.

*****

The investigation of confusion is a key.
By being clear about confusion,
One becomes cleared of confusion.

*****

My child, you are only
What you imagine yourself to be.
What you truly are is unimaginable.

*****

The true mystic does not confuse
What-Is with
What appears to be.
Knowing he knows nothing,
He is the incarnation of non-interference.

To run from what appears is
To be fearful.
To embrace whatever appears is
To be wise.
Those living at ease do not
Attempt to manipulate the world.

*****

Ignorance always requires support.
Pristine knowing,
Clear sight,
Stands free.

*****

Wu Hsin is the termite;
You are the chair.

*****

All that is needed is
Someone to explain that
No one is needed.

*****

Once it is seen that
One is not
A fragment of the whole, but rather
Wholeness itself,
The dramas that previously
Held so much power
Can no longer be found.

The One Substance is
The mother of all things.
She has many names,
None of which can touch her.

*****

What is sought is
Directly in front of the eyes, and
Directly behind the eyes.
There is nowhere it is not.
When the false boundaries called
In front and behind are
Seen as false,
Life loses all difficulty.

*****

Movement cannot be known when
There is no movement.
Yet, movement can only be known
From the background of no movement.

*****

The end of the path is
The understanding that
No path is necessary.
Then, one walks freely.

*****

Whereas the perceived is in constant flux,
That which perceives is immobile.
On which of the two the attention rests
Determines the point of view.
Thinking has value in the
Organizing of the known, but
It is not the tool with which
To approach the Great Mystery.

The Great Mystery can only be
Approached from silence.
It is, in fact,
The silence itself.

*****

That which perceives
The thinking and the feeling, is not
Identical to them.
This is the source of much confusion.

*****

The problems that appear in the mind are problems
Because they appear in the mind.
Viewed from outside of the mind,
They cannot be located.

*****

True knowledge requires no
Confirmation, affirmation or verification
From any outside source.
True knowledge is the knowledge that
There is no outside source.

*****

That which is ever-present and obvious is easily missed
When the attention rests on the transitory.
Returning is therefore a re-turning toward
The base of all things.

*****

Certainty is finite;
If everyone claims it,
No one can have it.

When it is fully apprehended that
Thinking is not the instrument that will
Take one to Understanding,
What is there to think about?

*****

The only difference between
A wise man and others is that
The wise man is no longer
Hoping for something to happen.

*****

It is a misunderstanding to believe that
One is not already
What one wants to become.
To see this clearly,
Brings becoming to an end.

*****

Those who chase two rabbits
Catch neither.

*****

The direct perception into What-Is results in
The loss of the desire to control time.
The wanting to extend the duration of happiness ends.
The wanting to shorten the duration of sorrow ends.
The fixation on what comes and goes ends as does
The preoccupation with longevity.
This rejection of time heralds
The onset of immortality.

To see a beginning in every ending and
An ending in every beginning is
To see eternity.

*****

Every day, become, at the least
One gram lighter.

*****

Water is not wetter in
One location than another.
There is no need to go there
To obtain what is also here.

*****

One step closer to
The attainment of peace is
The cessation of asking
Why?

*****

When the words are few,
The silence is great and
True listening begins.

*****

Clear sight is not an effect,
A result or a consequence.
There is therefore
Nothing to be done to cause it.

*****

Every effort adds another veil.

When one is comfortable with not knowing,
When one can live in seeming chaos,
The perfect order of things reveals itself.

$$*****$$

What could be more simple than to
Look in at what's looking out?

$$*****$$

The mystery of the Great Mystery is not
What it is, but
That it is.

$$*****$$

Fullness is
The purpose of emptiness.
The great gift is to see that
One is not a thing among things, but
The space in which all things are contained and
From where they emerge.

$$*****$$

One must say Yes
Even to one's
Inability to say Yes.

$$*****$$

Allow everything to be as it is,
Not seeking to improve it or
Correct it or
Remove it.
Then, what can be wrong with this moment?

Do not confuse
A man who is tired of sleeping with
One who is awake.

*****

Humility is not a trait of character.
It is an insight into the actual;
It is a knowing that
One knows nothing.

*****

The unmarked path
Extends from then and there to
Here and now.

*****

Wu Hsin's potion is
Comprised of equal parts of
Perceiving everything and
Identifying with nothing.

*****

Nothing can be added to
A bowl that is already full.
Emptied of everything,
Fullness is welcomed.

*****

Only fools believe that their god
Lives in their temple.
Where the god is not,
One is not.

Because one is no thing in particular,
One can never know what one is.
One can only know
What one is not.
This is good enough.

*****

Investigating the validity of the assumptions is
Easier than resolving the problems.

*****

When one is ready to have
Everything one thinks one knows
Turned upside down and,
Inside out,
Then, as if by magic,
Wu Hsin appears.

*****

Nothing brings satisfaction.
Nothing brings happiness.
Nothing brings contentment.
Nothing brings clarity.
Do nothing.

*****

Change your mind,
Change your world.

*****

Wu Hsin sees things as they are.
He does not try to control them.
They continue forward while
Wu Hsin remains at the center.

To dwell in what is personal
Impedes the realization of
The universal.
Understand that everything personal is merely
A collection of events
Happening to a centralized object,
A point of reference.
One is not the object.
What one is, is
The knowing of the object.
The pure functions of seeing,
Tasting,
Smelling,
Touching,
Hearing and
Thinking
Are not owned by anyone.
Yet, everyone claims them as their own.

*****

The primary desire is
The desire to be.
This births the world and its contents.

*****

That which remains unaffected by
The dissolution of the universe and the heavens is
The primary principle of being.
It is from this that
All arises and all returns.

Foo was a wise man and
Many came to sit with him from
Different provinces and different lands.
What was it that made Foo wise?
Foo was able to see through the limited to
The Unlimited.
He never saw individuals;
He only saw everything in everyone.

*****

The only thing
One ever sees is
One's own world.

*****

What is not needed
Drops off,
If it is not clung to.

*****

To pursue depth is to
Desire the infinite.
To pursue width is to be
Ensnared in the world.

*****

Many fear Wu Hsin.
Although he is old,
He can kill inside you that which
You so dearly hold to.

Life is not a search for wholeness.
It is the expression of it.
When this is apperceived,
Nothing need be changed.

*****

Visions may come.
Unique experiences may occur.
When they are completed,
Remember to clean the pig stall.

*****

One shackles oneself
To one's beliefs.
When the beliefs are removed,
The shackles are removed.
This is freedom.

*****

The natural state contains
Nothing that has been acquired.
When all the acquisitions have been dropped,
What is natural shines through.

*****

One's thoughts organize the world so well that
One is no longer able to see it.

*****

Clarity brings simplicity.
What complicates is discarded.
Those who sleep on the floor never
Fall from their bed.

Wisdom blossoms in direct proportion to
One's awareness of
One's own ignorance.
Seeing that one is not
As wise today as
One thought one was yesterday,
Makes one wiser today.

*****

Seeking relief is not the same as
Seeking a cure.
The former is transient whereas
The latter is forever.

*****

Go and stand in the water.
Immerse yourself in it,
Feeling its coolness.
Knowing its wetness.
In this manner,
One comes to understand its nature.
One can never know it
Seated in the oxcart.

*****

See that you are mistaken.
You call it night merely because
You have turned away from the sun.

*****

The only one who can
Tear down the wall is
The one who erected it.

Those who do not see clearly believe that
The sun wipes out the stars.
Those who know What-Is
Do not mistake illusion for reality.

*****

Loneliness is the
Byproduct of feeling separate.
Those who see that
They are not separate,
Never experience loneliness.
When the noise ceases,
Silence remains.
When thoughts of the past or future stop,
The present moment remains.
When thinking stops,
Clarity remains.
It is the emptying that
Allows the Silent-Clear-Presence to unfold.

*****

Once the pure taste of tea is known,
The tea may also be
Taken with milk or sugar.
Once knowing is clear,
Involvement in the world
Presents no problems.

*****

The seeing continues while
That which sees remains unseen.

*****

The solution to all problems is
To see who it is
Who has them.

Were yellow to appear on
A background of blue,
It would appear to be green.
Yellow can only be yellow when
It appears on a colorless background.
You are that background.
You are That.

*****

Wu Hsin's words are always brief.
Talking about eating
Doesn't satisfy the hunger.
These words merely point
To the restaurant.

Translations of Wu Hsin by Roy Melvyn

Aphorisms for Thirsty Fish
The Magnificence of the Ordinary
In the Shadow of the Formless
Recognition of the Obvious
No Great Future Attainment
Behind the Mind: The Short Discourses of Wu Hsin
Solving Yourself: Yuben de Wu Hsin
Being Conscious Presence

Made in United States
Troutdale, OR
05/17/2025

31441109R00076